P9-DFZ-925

Strange ... But True?

CROP CIRCLES

KYLA STEINKRAUS

BLACK
RABBIT
BOOKS

Bolt is published by Black Rabbit Books
P.O. Box 3263, Mankato, Minnesota, 56002.
www.blackrabbitbooks.com
Copyright © 2018 Black Rabbit Books

Marysa Storm, editor; Grant Gould, interior
designer; Michael Sellner, cover designer;
Omay Ayres, photo researcher

All rights reserved. No part of this book may be reproduced, stored in a
retrieval system or transmitted in any form or by any means, electronic,
mechanical, photocopying, recording, or otherwise, without written
permission from the publisher.

Library of Congress Cataloging-in-Publication Data
Names: Steinkraus, Kyla, author.
Title: Crop circles / by Kyla Steinkraus.
Other titles: Bolt (North Mankato, Minn.) | Strange ... but true? (Series)
Description: Mankato, Minnesota : Black Rabbit Books, [2018] | Series: Bolt |
Series: Strange ... but true? | Includes bibliographical references and index.
Identifiers: LCCN 2016050039 (print) | LCCN 2016054060 (ebook) | ISBN
9781680721829 (library binding) | ISBN 9781680722468 (e-book) | ISBN
9781680724790 (paperback)
Subjects: LCSH: Crop circles–Juvenile literature. | Curiosities and
wonders–Juvenile literature.
Classification: LCC AG244 .S74 2018 (print) | LCC AG244 (ebook) | DDC
001.94–dc23
LC record available at https://lccn.loc.gov/2016050039

Printed in the United States at CG Book Printers,
North Mankato, Minnesota, 56003. 3/17

Lakeview Public Library
3 6645 00117974 6

Image Credits
Adobe Stock: Luca Oleas-
tri, Cover; Alamy: Dale O'Dell,
6–7, 20 (field), 26; Dennis Halli-
nan, Cover; John Henshall, 15; Peter
Widmann, 11; iStock: Georgethefourth,
19; Newscom: Mirrorpix, 22; Shutter-
stock: abramsdesign, 4–5; andrea crisante,
16–17; aslysun, 12 (bottom); canbedone, 1,
32, Back Cover; daulon, 31; Lena_graphics,
20 (alien); NikolayN, 28–29; solarseven, 3;
Temporary Temples: Steve Alexander, 8–9,
12, 25
Every effort has been made to contact
copyright holders for material reproduced in this book. Any omissions
will be rectified in subsequent
printings if notice is given
to the publisher.

Contents

CHAPTER 1

A

Mystery

It was a fall morning. Edwin Fuhr worked in a field. Suddenly, he noticed something weird. He saw five strange shapes **hovering** above the field. They looked like silver bowls turned upside down. They began to spin. Then they shot up and into the sky. They left behind five flat circles in the field.

5

Many Questions

Were those strange shapes spaceships? Did aliens make the marks in the field?

Crop circles are designs that appear in fields. Some are simple circles. Others are large patterns. No one really knows where they come from. Some people think aliens make them. Others think there's a down-to-earth explanation.

CROPS BENT IN SWIRL PATTERN

FLATTENED STALKS

MADE MOSTLY AT NIGHT

HAPPENS IN FIELDS OF WHEAT, RYE, CORN, AND BARLEY

CLEAN EDGES

PLANTS KEEP GROWING

NO TRACKS

Crop circles appear in the summer. They last until farmers harvest the crops. **Tourists** travel to see them. Visitors come from all over the world.

Some farmers charge a **fee** to see the circles. Others don't want the tourists. They mow over the circles.

More than 10,000 people visited the Julia Set crop circle.

11

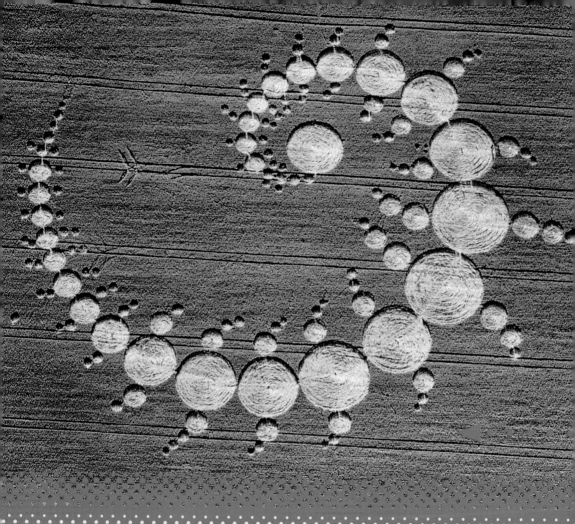

Stonehenge is a stone circle. It is in England. Some people believe it has magic powers. Many crop circles appear near similar places.

Famous Circles

In 1990, a circle appeared in Alton Barnes in England. It was one of the first crop circles to use multiple shapes. Thousands of people went to see it.

In 1996, a circle formed near Stonehenge. It was called the Julia Set. It appeared during the day. **Witnesses** say it formed in only 30 minutes. The spiral was 900 feet (274 meters) long. The design had more than 140 circles.

CHAPTER 2

History of

Before the 1970s, few people reported crop circles. Today, people find hundreds of circles every year. Years ago, crop circles had simple designs. Now, they are larger. They're also more **complex**.

CROP CIRCLE SIGHTINGS BY DECADE

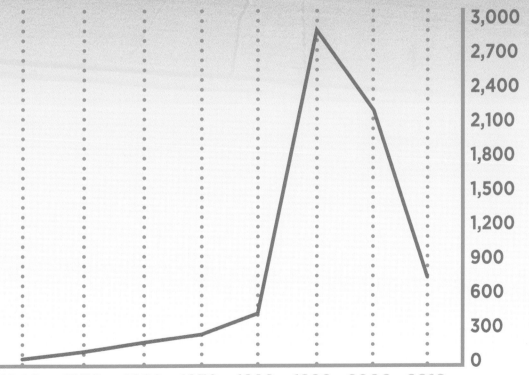

							3,000
							2,700
							2,400
							2,100
							1,800
							1,500
							1,200
							900
							600
							300
							0

1940s 1950s 1960s 1970s 1980s 1990s 2000s 2010s
(UP TO 2015)

POPULAR CROP CIRCLE SITES

Crop circles form all around the world. But some places get more. About 85 to 90 percent of circles appear in England.

CANADA

ENGLAND

UNITED STATES

NETHERLANDS

GERMANY

ITALY

CHAPTER 3

UFOs

in the Corn

Some people don't believe humans made all crop circles. They think some circles were too hard for humans to make in one night.

People who study crop circles have a name. They are called cereologists.

19

Reasons to Believe

Believers think crop circles are made by aliens. They say the circles are from spaceships. Some people believe the circles have special energy.

Witnesses support those **claims**. They say they've seen strange lights near the circles. Some have seen flying objects. Others have felt dizzy or sick. They've heard weird crackling noises.

Crop artists use rope and flat boards to make their circles. They tie a piece of rope to each end of a board. They use the board to flatten crops. This tool is called a stalk stomper.

CHAPTER 4

Crop Circle Hoaxes

Skeptics believe people make all crop circles. In 1991, Doug Bower and Dave Chorley said they faked around 200 circles.

Other people make crop circles as art. They call themselves crop artists. Many crop artists make circles in secret at night.

The Golden Ball Formation

In 2005, a circle in Wiltshire, England, formed. People called it the Golden Ball formation. It was 96 feet (29 m) wide. Years later, people asked a group to re-create the circle. The group made it in about four hours. This test proved people could make circles quickly.

People who believe circles aren't made by humans are called croppies.

25

What's Really Happening?

Some people think all circles are human-made. They say people can make perfect shapes with the right tools.

Believers say people couldn't make large circles so quickly. They wonder why there are no tracks in the fields. And they believe witnesses' stories.

Will we ever learn the truth?

Believe It or Not?

Answer the questions below.
Then add up your points to
see if you believe.

1 **You see strange lights in the sky.
What do you think?**

A. The aliens are coming for me!
(3 points)

B. What is that? (2 points)

C. It must be a plane. (1 point)

2. Look at the pictures in this book again. What's your first thought?

A. People couldn't have made those. (3 points)

B. Who or what made those? (2 points)

C. Those crop artists did a great job. (1 point)

3. You see a strange circle in a field. What do you think?

A. Humans couldn't have made that. (3 points)

B. That's a little odd. (2 points)

C. Someone had fun in the field! (1 point)

· · · · · · · · · · · · · ·

3 points
There's no way aliens make crop circles.

4-8 points
Maybe aliens make them. Maybe they don't.

9 points
You're a total croppie!

claim (KLAYM)—to say something is true when some people might say it's not true

complex (KOM-pleks)—connected in complicated ways

crop (KROP)—a plant or plant product that is grown by farmers

fee (FEE)—an amount of money that must be paid

hovering (HUHV-er-ing)—floating in the air without moving any direction

skeptic (SKEP-tik)—a person who questions something

tourist (TOOR-ist)—a person who travels for fun

witness (WIT-nes)—someone who sees something happen

BOOKS

Lassieur, Allison. *Are Crop Circles Real?* Unexplained: What's the Evidence? Mankato, MN: Amicus High Interest, 2016.

Noll, Elizabeth. *UFOs.* Strange ... But True? Mankato, MN: Black Rabbit Books, 2017.

O'Keefe, Emily. *Crop Circles.* Unsolved Mysteries. Mankato, MN: Child's World, 2015.

WEBSITES

Are We Alone?
www.timeforkids.com/news/are-we-alone/203396

Crop Circles Database
www.cropcirclesdatabase.com

Do Aliens Really Exist?
discoverykids.com/articles/do-aliens-really-exist/

INDEX